AS YOU DE᠎ ᠎ ᠎

for
Jonathan Kent

Luigi Pirandello
AS YOU DESIRE ME

A new version by Hugh Whitemore

Literal translation by Gwenda Pandolfi

OBERON BOOKS
LONDON

First published in this version in 2005 by Oberon Books Ltd.
521 Caledonian Road, London N7 9RH
Tel: 020 7607 3637 / Fax: 020 7607 3629
e-mail: info@oberonbooks.com
www.oberonbooks.com

Cover design by aka; photography by Hugo Glendinning

ISBN: 1 84002 584 0

Printed in Great Britain by Antony Rowe Ltd, Chippenham.

Characters

L'IGNOTA

MOP

SALTER

THREE MEN

BOFFI

BRUNO

SALESIO

LENA

INES

SILVIO

MADWOMAN

NUN

This version of *As You Desire Me* was first performed at the Playhouse Theatre, London on 27 October 2005 (previews from 21 October) with the following cast:

L'IGNOTA, Kristin Scott Thomas

SALTER, Bob Hoskins

LENA, Margaret Tyzack

SALESIO, John Carlisle

BRUNO, Richard Lintern

BOFFI, Finbar Lynch

INES, Tessa Churchard

SILVIO, Andrew Woodall

MOP, Hannah Young

MADWOMAN, Stephanie Jacob

NUN, Katherine Stark

THREE MEN, Richard Trinder, Charlie Walker-Wise, Tim Delap

Director Jonathan Kent

Designer Paul Brown

Lighting Mark Henderson

Sound Paul Groothuis

Music Tim Sutton

A dazzling white spotlight slices down through the darkness onto a beautiful night-club entertainer in her thirties: L'IGNOTA ('The Unknown Woman'). Voluptuous in an evening gown, she sings a German cabaret song of 1930. This is the Berlin of George Grosz and Otto Dix, of decadence and danger.

Blackout.

Lights up on the living room of Carl Salter's flat in Berlin. Night. An archway leads to the entrance hall. Beyond, the study. Sombre Teutonic decorations and furniture. Uncanny and mysterious.

A girl, MOP, lies huddled on a chair. Her hair is cut like a boy's. She is wearing black silk pyjamas. She might be asleep. In fact, she is weeping.

Her father, CARL SALTER, enters swiftly from the study. He is in his fifties; sensual, powerfully built; cropped grey hair; wearing an expensive dressing gown. He is upset and agitated.

SALTER: She's coming back with them! Those drunks from the nightclub!

He is holding a small revolver.

MOP: What've you got there?

SALTER: Bloody bitch!

MOP: Papa – don't –

SALTER: Night after goddam night! I've had enough –

MOP: No, Papa – please!

SALTER: – more than enough!

MOP: Stop, Papa – don't!

SALTER: Bitch! She does it deliberately –

He hurries to the hall.

MOP: Put that gun away!

SALTER: They're coming upstairs – Listen! – stupid pansy voices!

MOP: Don't, Papa – please –

SALTER: Vermin!

MOP: PAPA!

SALTER: I won't put up with it – why the hell should I? – without me she'd be nothing –

The front door bursts open.

L'IGNOTA comes in followed by THREE MEN in evening dress. L'IGNOTA is wearing an elegant cloak over her evening gown.

A fourth man, BOFFI, follows them, standing some distance apart.

L'IGNOTA: Hello, Salter. Look what I've got. Young ones. Lucky me.

The FIRST MAN tries to grab L'IGNOTA.

FIRST MAN: (*Singing.*) Sex-Appeal – Sex-Appeal…

L'IGNOTA: – Sniffing around like dogs on heat. Leave me alone.

THIRD MAN: But you said – you promised –

L'IGNOTA: You shouldn't believe a lady like me.

FIRST MAN: (*Singing.*) – Sex-Appeal –

SECOND MAN: I want a drink – where's the champagne?

FIRST MAN: (*Singing.*) Sex-Appeal – Sex-Appeal…

SALTER: Get out of here! All of you!

SECOND MAN: Champagne, champagne, I want champagne!

He tries to grab L'IGNOTA by the arm.

L'IGNOTA: (*Pushing him away.*) Go away! Leave me alone!

SECOND MAN: I want a drink.

L'IGNOTA: Not funny anymore. Shoo, shoo, shoo!

SALTER: You heard what she said. Out!

THIRD MAN: She invited us. We're her guests!

SALTER: Get the hell out of here!

SECOND MAN: One more drink!

FIRST MAN: (*Singing.*) Sex-Appeal – Sex-Appeal…

He seizes L'IGNOTA, trying to tear off her cloak. MOP tries to intervene.

MOP: Don't do that! Stop it!

L'IGNOTA: (*To MOP.*) Stop mauling me!

SALTER: (*Grabbing the SECOND MAN.*) All of you – OUT!

SALTER brandishes his revolver.

SECOND MAN: My God, he's got a gun!

SALTER: I'll count to three –

THIRD MAN: We're going, we're going!

SALTER: One! –

SECOND MAN: (*To his companions, as he heads for the door.*) Come on, come on!

SALTER: Two! –

THIRD MAN: All right, we're going –

SECOND MAN: (*To SALTER.*) You sad old bastard.

The THREE MEN tumble out of the flat. The FIRST MAN is still singing:

FIRST MAN: Sex-Appeal – Sex-Appeal…

During the confusion, BOFFI has retreated into a shadowy corner.

SALTER: (*As he slams the front door.*) For God's sake, Elma.

L'IGNOTA: For God's sake what?

SALTER: I will not have those parasites in my apartment. Vermin.

L'IGNOTA: Shut up, Salter.

She goes to pour herself a brandy.

SALTER: I'm telling you, I'm warning you –

L'IGNOTA: I'll do what I like.

SALTER: You'll do as you're told.

L'IGNOTA: Don't try to bully me.

SALTER: You slut.

L'IGNOTA: You want me to go? – Fine, all right, that's fine by me – fine, fine, I'll go –

She puts down her glass and heads for the door.

MOP: Don't, Elma, please.

L'IGNOTA: You heard him. I'm a slut. He wants me out. Fine, I'll go.

SALTER: I will not have you bringing that scum to my apartment.

L'IGNOTA: (*She opens the door and calls to the departing revellers.*) Wait for me – wait!

MOP: Stop! – don't!

L'IGNOTA: You don't own me, Salter. I'm not your slave. (*Calling.*) Wait! I'm coming!

MOP: DON'T!

BOFFI steps forward from the shadows.

BOFFI: Lucia!

L'IGNOTA stops and stares at him. She closes the front door. SALTER and MOP are also staring at BOFFI. He is in his forties; wearing evening dress.

L'IGNOTA: Who the hell are you?

BOFFI: I am a friend, Lucia.

SALTER: Get out of here!

BOFFI: You don't understand –

SALTER: (*Grabbing him by the arm.*) OUT!

BOFFI: Let me explain –

SALTER: OUT!

BOFFI: (*Freeing himself.*) I'm not with them.

SALTER: Liar. I saw you from the window.

L'IGNOTA: No! – he's telling the truth. He's not with them.

MOP: (*To L'IGNOTA.*) Who is he?

L'IGNOTA: I've no idea.

BOFFI: Tell them, Lucia – (*To MOP and SALTER.*) – she knows who I am.

MOP: Her name's not Lucia.

SALTER: (*To L'IGNOTA.*) Who is he?

L'IGNOTA: I don't know! I saw him outside the club. He's been following me.

MOP: Following you…?

L'IGNOTA: All this week.

BOFFI: Lucia…

L'IGNOTA: Every night he's followed me home. I could hear his voice, 'Lucia, Lucia,' like a parrot, 'Lucia! Lucia!'

BOFFI: And every night you looked round.

L'IGNOTA: Because I heard you calling.

BOFFI: Because you heard your name.

L'IGNOTA: When somebody calls out you look round –

BOFFI: You looked round because your name is Lucia –

L'IGNOTA: (*To MOP and SALTER.*) This is just nonsense.

BOFFI: – Lucia Pieri.

L'IGNOTA: (*To BOFFI.*) You're talking nonsense.

BOFFI: (*To SALTER.*) I saw her photograph outside the nightclub. Five days ago. I couldn't believe my eyes. Lucia. Here, in Berlin. I waited outside the club – (*Turning to L'IGNOTA.*) – and yes, you're right, I did follow you. I had to be sure.

SALTER: Lucia what? Perry?

BOFFI: Pieri. Italian. Her husband's name is Bruno Pieri.

SALTER: Her husband?!

L'IGNOTA: (*To SALTER.*) He's mad.

BOFFI: Your husband is here, Lucia.

L'IGNOTA: Here? Where?

SALTER: Her husband's dead.

BOFFI: I spoke to him this evening.

L'IGNOTA: That's impossible.

BOFFI: He's staying at the Bismarck. Five minutes walk away.

L'IGNOTA: I have no husband.

BOFFI: Phone him. Call the Bismarck Hotel. Speak to him.

L'IGNOTA laughs.

L'IGNOTA: (*Mocking.*) So I have a husband! Just round the corner at the Bismarck Hotel! This is ridiculous!

BOFFI: I sent for him as soon as I saw your photograph.

L'IGNOTA: You're mad!

BOFFI: I sent him a telegram.

SALTER: (*To BOFFI.*) She's right, you're mad. (*Brandishing his revolver.*) Get out before I call the police.

L'IGNOTA steps forward.

L'IGNOTA: No, wait! Wait!

SALTER: Wait? Wait for what?

L'IGNOTA: Wait for… (*She hesitates for a moment, half-smiling.*) Well. I mean. Suppose he's not mad – suppose – suppose –

SALTER: Suppose *what*…?

L'IGNOTA: Suppose I am this – ?

BOFFI: Lucia Pieri.

L'IGNOTA: Lucia Pieri. I could be. It's possible.

SALTER: You're drunk.

L'IGNOTA: (*Teasing him.*) All right – if I'm not Lucia Pieri, who am I?

SALTER: Who are you…?

L'IGNOTA: This man says he knows me – do you know me any better?

SALTER: Do I know you…? Ha! I know you better than you know yourself.

L'IGNOTA: Well that's not difficult. (*To BOFFI.*) I have no memory. None. I have no idea who I really am or what my life has been. The last four years is all I can remember. Before that – nothing. (*Turning to MOP.*) Tell him my name.

MOP: Elma.

L'IGNOTA: Elma!

MOP: It's Arabic. It means water.

L'IGNOTA: Water – silvery, rippling water… (*She makes a rippling movement with her fingers; then, a change of tone.*) God, my head is spinning. I've drunk too much. (*To MOP.*) Be a good girl. Fetch me something to eat.

MOP: What do you want?

L'IGNOTA: I don't know. Anything. I'm starving.

MOP: Shall I make you a sandwich?

L'IGNOTA: Anything.

MOP goes.

SALTER: (*To BOFFI.*) You've made a stupid mistake. Get the hell out of here.

L'IGNOTA: Don't speak to him like that.

BOFFI: The Signora knows I have not made a mistake.

L'IGNOTA: (*To BOFFI.*) I don't want you to tell him that you've found me.

BOFFI: But he has waited and searched –

SALTER: (*To L'IGNOTA.*) What are you talking about? You said your husband was dead.

BOFFI: She lied.

SALTER: (*To L'IGNOTA.*) Did you?

L'IGNOTA: Yes, Salter – I lied! (*She laughs.*) Let's swap lies, shall we? I'll tell you the lies I've told you and you can tell me the lies you've told me.

SALTER: I don't lie to you.

L'IGNOTA: (*She laughs.*) Oh, Salter!

SALTER: I swear to you…

L'IGNOTA: You even lie to yourself. So what? We all do it all the time. If the truth doesn't suit us, we change it. All right, it may be true. Perhaps somebody close to me did die. Perhaps it was my husband, perhaps not. But whoever he was it doesn't matter, because he was married to someone who no longer exists. (*To BOFFI.*) So tell us about him. Tell us the story of this poor widower who's come to Berlin to find his long-lost Signora Lucia.

BOFFI: I think we should talk in private.

L'IGNOTA: Oh, no – here. Here, in front of Salter. I want him to know everything. We have no secrets here, no taboos.

SALTER: Just like animals.

L'IGNOTA: Yes, but animals can't help themselves, can they? – it's their nature – (*MOP enters with a plate of sandwiches.*) Thank you, Mop. How clever you are.

MOP: Look at your dress.

L'IGNOTA: What?

MOP: Your dress. It's torn.

L'IGNOTA: Must've been those bastards at the club.

MOP: I can mend it.

L'IGNOTA: (*To BOFFI, ignoring MOP.*) I've had too much to drink. As always. Did you know that Lucia – I hope her husband won't be too shocked – Signora Lucia sings and dances in a nightclub. The 'Lari-Fari'. Oh but of course you know that; you saw my photograph outside. When I say 'sings and dances' that's really – what d'you call it, what's the word? – a polite way of saying something unpleasant – a euphemism! – when I say I sing and dance that's actually a euphemism – what I really do, what I'm paid to do, is to arouse the customers – ask him, (*Referring to SALTER.*) he knows it's true – in fact, he rather likes it – he likes the idea of going to bed with a woman whose profession is sexual arousal. Don't you, Salter? You enjoy it. It makes you feel powerful. Potent. (*Drawing closer to BOFFI.*) Well…? Do you still believe I'm the woman you think I am?

BOFFI: Yes, you've changed – but surprisingly little when you consider what's happened to you.

L'IGNOTA: So what did happen to me? Come along, let's talk about the past. It comes in so many shapes and sizes. (*Pointing to SALTER and MOP.*) There are two of them. Look. (*She laughs.*) If only you knew…

SALTER: Shut up! – you're drunk – you'll be ashamed tomorrow morning –

MOP: (*Interrupting, to SALTER.*) You're the one who should be ashamed. Dearest Elma –

She goes to embrace L'IGNOTA.

L'IGNOTA: Go away, Mop! – leave me alone!

SALTER: Yes, leave her alone. Go to bed.

L'IGNOTA: (*To MOP.*) Make me another sandwich.

MOP: Will you come and eat it in the kitchen?

L'IGNOTA: Why? – so you can kiss me?

SALTER laughs.

MOP: (*To SALTER.*) Pig! I hate you!

L'IGNOTA: (*To SALTER.*) Stop it! (*To BOFFI.*) They're jealous of each other.

MOP: Please don't say that –

L'IGNOTA: Look at them! Father and daughter. Can you believe it?

MOP: (*Agonised.*) – please.

L'IGNOTA: (*A mocking laugh.*) Ha! – look at him. Pathetic! His wife won't divorce him, so –

SALTER: (*Enraged.*) God – I've had enough of this!

L'IGNOTA: – so she sends their daughter to get him away from me. What happens? The daughter falls in love with me. Can you imagine anything more absurd?

MOP: (*To L'IGNOTA.*) Be careful. He's got a gun.

L'IGNOTA: Have you, Salter?

SALTER takes the revolver out of his pocket and puts it on a table.

SALTER: There.

L'IGNOTA: Is it loaded?

SALTER: It is.

L'IGNOTA: Is the bullet for me – or for you?

SALTER: The choice is yours, my dear.

L'IGNOTA picks up the revolver.

MOP: Elma! – don't!

BOFFI: Put it down, Lucia – don't be foolish.

L'IGNOTA: (*Replacing the revolver, then to BOFFI.*) Comedy or tragedy – which do you prefer? We can provide both in this household.

SALTER: (*A shout.*) Stop this – stop it! (*Silence; L'IGNOTA stares at SALTER.*) You said you'd give it all up. You promised.

L'IGNOTA: Did I?

SALTER: You said you'd make a decision. About us.

L'IGNOTA: (*Mocking him.*) About 'us'…? Why, Herr Salter, what *do* you mean?

SALTER: Don't pretend you've forgotten.

L'IGNOTA: All right, let's make a decision. (*Gestures to revolver.*) With that…?

SALTER: You haven't got the nerve.

L'IGNOTA: That's where you're wrong. (*She picks up the revolver and points it at SALTER.*) Don't you believe me? Do you want me to? Do you? (*Lowers revolver.*) Oh God – I'm so tired of all this. (*Goes to SALTER.*) Why don't I – instead of killing you – kiss you – one kiss. (*She kisses him on the lips.*) Nothing to say…? Not even thank you? (*Gives him the revolver.*) Your turn. Kill me if you want to.

MOP: No, don't – he'll do it, he'll shoot!

L'IGNOTA: Let him, I don't give a damn. (*Gazing at SALTER.*) God, Salter – I wish you had the courage… (*To BOFFI.*) It's true what I say. I'm at the end of the road, the end of the line, the end of my – what d'you call it? – tether. I'm at the end of my tether, whatever that may be – have you any idea what it feels like to be at the end of your tether? Well, I'm there. I've reached that point. And I'm starving. Famished. Get me another sandwich, Mop.

MOP goes.

BOFFI: (*To L'IGNOTA.*) Let me help you.

SALTER goes to BOFFI.

SALTER: Now look – this is my apartment. I want you to leave. Now.

BOFFI: I am here because of the Signora.

SALTER: The Signora is a guest in my house!

L'IGNOTA: But not a prisoner. I'm allowed to ask friends to visit me.

SALTER: Friends…? You said you didn't know him. (*To BOFFI.*) Get out.

BOFFI: Only if the lady comes with me.

L'IGNOTA: Then I shall.

SALTER: You will not.

L'IGNOTA: Stop me.

SALTER: Very well.

L'IGNOTA: By force?

SALTER: If necessary. (*Grasping her by the wrist.*) For God's sake, Elma – this man is a complete stranger! What the hell are you trying to do?

BOFFI: The Signora *does* know me. She's just pretending not to recognise me.

MOP: (*Entering, with a sandwich on a plate.*) So who are you?

BOFFI: My name is Boffi.

L'IGNOTA: The photographer?

BOFFI: (*To SALTER.*) There, you see? – she does know me.

SALTER: She knows your name – so do I. We saw an exhibition –

MOP: There were pictures in the paper –

L'IGNOTA: I do know him. I was lying. He's a friend of my husband's.

SALTER: Your husband's…? But you said –

L'IGNOTA: (*Freeing herself from SALTER's grasp.*) Let go of me!

SALTER: Why are you doing this?

L'IGNOTA: I didn't want him to find out what had happened to me.

BOFFI: You mean Bruno?

L'IGNOTA: Yes.

BOFFI: But he knows already.

L'IGNOTA: Knows what?

BOFFI: Everything.

L'IGNOTA: How?

BOFFI: He asked questions, followed all the leads, collected every scrap of evidence.

SALTER: Evidence?

BOFFI: Prima facie, circumstantial, eye-witness accounts, anything he could find. The place is full of it.

L'IGNOTA: What place…?

BOFFI: The villa, of course.

SALTER: What villa?

L'IGNOTA: My villa! Where I lived. (*To BOFFI.*) All right. Tell him – (*Indicating SALTER.*) – tell him everything. This animal took advantage of me when I was desperate. Tell him what happened to me. Every detail. Rub his face in it. (*BOFFI hesitates.*) Come on! Tell him!

BOFFI: She was – she was alone in the house.

L'IGNOTA: That's right. Alone.

BOFFI: It was in the afternoon. Late.

L'IGNOTA: Almost evening. Shadows on the terrace.

BOFFI: The old gardener heard her screaming. Filippo.

L'IGNOTA: Filippo! Yes!

BOFFI: There was nothing he could do. The soldiers ransacked the house. They found where she was hiding. Forced themselves upon her. All of them – all of them. How could she possibly protect herself? When we came back – the ruins, the desolation, the horrors of invasion – we knew what must've happened…

L'IGNOTA: The invasion! (*Triumphantly, to SALTER.*) I told you! Don't you remember? I told you about the invasion!

SALTER: (*Disconcerted, having to agree.*) Yes, yes, you did say something…

L'IGNOTA: It was my house. I lived there.

BOFFI: Near Venice.

L'IGNOTA: Near Venice. With my husband.

BOFFI: (*To SALTER.*) Bruno Pieri was a young Italian officer – gallant, courageous. He came back after the war to find the estate in ruins. Everything gone. His life destroyed. No trace of his young wife. They'd been married for just a year.

L'IGNOTA: Bruno…

BOFFI: He always called you Cia.

L'IGNOTA: Cia! – yes, Cia…

BOFFI: The thought of what might've happened to you drove him mad. Literally – demented. He was mad for more than a year. He searched everywhere. He was haunted by the thought – obsessed – he thought the soldiers had carried you off and used you as their whore.

L'IGNOTA: Yes, yes. That's what happened.

SALTER: Wait. I read something…

BOFFI: Yes, it was in the papers.

SALTER: About this woman who disappeared.

BOFFI: Bruno arranged for it to be published.

L'IGNOTA: When was this? I didn't see it.

SALTER: Of course you saw it! We talked about it. (*To BOFFI.*) A friend of mine knew of a similar case – a doctor friend in Austria, a psychiatrist – he told us about it – (*To L'IGNOTA.*) – and you – yes, of course you read it! – (*He pauses, staring at L'IGNOTA.*) Ah! I see! – I see what you're trying to do – you're trying to pass yourself off as this Italian woman, this Lucia –

BOFFI: She is Lucia. I'm sure of it. I've known her since she was a child.

L'IGNOTA: (*To SALTER.*) Since I was a child – you see?

BOFFI: I have.

SALTER: Doesn't matter how long. I've sacrificed my life for you.

L'IGNOTA: I didn't ask you to.

SALTER: I left my wife – I destroyed our marriage because of you.

L'IGNOTA: Because of lust, Salter.

SALTER: You tricked me.

L'IGNOTA: Why not? Life has tricked me, darling. You heard what he (*Meaning BOFFI.*) said. The war, the invasion, the soldiers. Why shouldn't I trick you?

SALTER: Stop it, Elma, for God's sake. Stop this ridiculous charade.

BOFFI: This is no charade.

L'IGNOTA: Even if it is, so what? You're my saviour, Boffi. Sent by the gods to help me. Tell me about my childhood. I want to know everything. I was a different person then – everything was different – like a dream.

BOFFI: Yes, Cia – the past *is* a kind of dream.

L'IGNOTA: Ah! – you call me Cia too – does everyone call me Cia? – do they? – I thought – hoped – it was only him – only Bruno who called me that.

SALTER: What the hell are you playing at? You can't just dump me like this –

L'IGNOTA: I can do what I like.

SALTER: No, you cannot! Not after the way you trapped me –

L'IGNOTA: (*Laughing.*) I trapped you…?!

SALTER: What else would you call it?

L'IGNOTA: I seduced you, Salter. You shouldn't have let yourself be seduced.

SALTER: You deceived me. Heartless bitch.

L'IGNOTA: We deceived each other. (*To BOFFI.*) Look at him. Carl Salter. The famous writer. He may sell thousands of copies, but he's a joke – a hack! (*Taking BOFFI by the arm.*) Come on, let's go. (*To SALTER.*) We're going for a walk, Signor Boffi and I. We'll talk about my childhood. Cia's childhood. If you want to stop me, why don't you take that revolver and shoot me dead? Wouldn't that be fun? Come on, Salter – try it – Bang bang! – why don't you?

SALTER: Don't tempt me.

L'IGNOTA: Well here I am. I've been through the war. I know all about guns and shooting. (*To BOFFI.*) He won't do it because he's too much of a coward. He hasn't got the nerve.

SALTER: Oh yes I have – and well you know it.

L'IGNOTA: You're a clown, Salter. I despise you. (*Sudden desperation.*) God, I can't stand it any longer! (*To BOFFI.*) – this life – the insanity of it – the shouting, the screaming – everything spinning, my head spinning – every vice, every perversion – everyone searching for a gratification they can never find! (*Pointing at SALTER.*) Look at him! Bloated like a corpse! And me. Look at me! These clothes! The clothes of a whore! Look at the city – the whole of Berlin – a vision of hell – a lunatic asylum. (*Pointing at MOP.*) And her!

Look at her! (*Drawing closer to BOFFI.*) I came home one night. Late. I was drunk. I'd been at the club, so what do you expect? – I got back here – blood all over her face (*Referring to MOP.*) – scratched from here to here – (*Forehead to cheek gesture.*) God knows what had happened – look, you can still see the scar.

SALTER: I didn't touch her.

MOP: I did it myself – I told you – why don't you believe me?

L'IGNOTA: I've no idea what happened. I was so drunk I don't remember which one of them took me to bed. (*Agonised.*) God – God – God! – I've got to get away from here –

BOFFI: Then come with me.

L'IGNOTA: I've got to get away from myself – from the creature I've become – I can't go on like this.

BOFFI: Another life is waiting for you. Your real life as Lucia. Bruno is waiting for you.

L'IGNOTA turns and stares at BOFFI.

L'IGNOTA: He's still waiting…? – after ten years? – still hoping…?

BOFFI: Still waiting for his beloved wife…

SALTER: (*With contempt.*) His Cia…

BOFFI: Yes – his Cia. People thought she was dead. It suited them to believe that. But he refused to listen. He always believed you were alive. He knew it!

L'IGNOTA: But how – I mean why – if she's still alive why hasn't she gone back to him?

BOFFI: Because he felt that after all the terrible things that had happened to her – to you –

L'IGNOTA: The woman he's looking for no longer exists.

BOFFI: – he believed – believes – that you haven't gone back because you're afraid.

L'IGNOTA: Of what?

BOFFI: Afraid you could never be the same to him after what happened. The degradation, the abuse…

L'IGNOTA: Does he believe I *could* be the same?

BOFFI: He does.

L'IGNOTA: Do *you* think so?

BOFFI: Yes. If you choose to be.

SALTER: Elma – don't do this!

L'IGNOTA: (*To BOFFI, ignoring SALTER.*) The same – after ten years? He's crazy. That's impossible.

BOFFI: Yes, but now – if you want to –

L'IGNOTA: If I want to…! God! To put all this behind me! No memories, no shame, no guilt! Look at me – look at this face. You say it's hers? Is that what you're saying? Perhaps you're right – perhaps I am just a body without a name – left luggage – waiting for someone to come and claim it. All right! Let him have me. If he can breathe new life into this body – if he can create his Cia out of me, then let him do it – let him have me!

BOFFI: I'll phone him at once.

SALTER: *I'll* phone him. I'll phone him from the study. Then we shall see…

L'IGNOTA: You're being very accommodating, Salter.
   Why, I wonder? (*To BOFFI.*) You have to be careful with
   Salter – can't trust him an inch – (*Calling to SALTER.*)
   – can you, Salter? (*Going to drinks table.*) Let's have a
   drink. (*To BOFFI.*) What would you like? Not her, of
   course – (*Referring to MOP.*) – she's far too young.

   *MOP suddenly realises what her father intends to do. She
   runs after him.*

MOP: Oh God! – Papa – PAPA, DON'T!

   *A revolver shot. MOP throws open the study door. SALTER is
   lying beside his desk. L'IGNOTA and BOFFI follow MOP.*

   Oh God oh God oh God! (*She flings herself down beside
   SALTER.*) He's done it. He's killed himself.

BOFFI: (*Kneeling beside SALTER.*) No, he's not dead. He's
   still breathing.

MOP: There's blood coming out of his mouth.

BOFFI: We should lift his head –

MOP: Let me do it. Oh Papa, Papa… (*Grasping her father
   by the hand.*) It's me, Papa – it's Mop… (*To BOFFI.*) Give
   me that cushion.

BOFFI: We must get him to a doctor.

   SALTER groans and tries to speak.

MOP: What is it, Papa? What are you trying to say? (*To
   L'IGNOTA.*) He's looking at you.

BOFFI: A doctor –

MOP: Yes.

BOFFI: (*Heading for the door.*) I'll go and ask –

MOP: There's a doctor living here. Dr Schultz. His flat's on the second floor.

BOFFI: Dr Schultz. Second floor. Good.

BOFFI exits. MOP is cradling SALTER's head on her lap.

MOP: He's asking for you. He needs you. Elma…

L'IGNOTA ignores her. She walks into the living room and pours herself a brandy.

You can't leave him now – you can't – not now.

L'IGNOTA drinks. Lights begin to fade around her. She sings to herself the cabaret song from the opening scene.

The front door is thrown open. A man, BRUNO, stands silhouetted in a shaft of brilliant light. L'IGNOTA turns and looks at him.

L'IGNOTA: A body without a name – without a name…

BRUNO: Cia! Cia!

Lights fade to black.

In the darkness, the sound of an Italian church bell.

Lights up. The loggia of a large villa in northern Italy. There is a marble balustrade with slender columns supporting a glass-paned roof. Beyond, a green landscape bathed in the cool, clear light one sees in a painting by Piero della Francesca. A staircase leads to the upper floors. At the foot of the staircase there is a large oval portrait in oils of Lucia Pieri as she was when newly married.

SALESIO comes in from the garden. He is in his sixties, wearing an old-fashioned cream suit and carrying a bunch of roses.

LENA comes down the stairs; she is about sixty, stout and grey-haired, dressed in black. She stares disapprovingly.

LENA: For God's sake, Salesio!

SALESIO: What…?

LENA: Look at you! All dressed up. It's not a wedding.

SALESIO: Well I thought –

LENA: You're a fool!

She seizes the roses.

SALESIO: I wanted it to be nice.

LENA: (*Contempt.*) Nice!

SALESIO: For Cia.

LENA: You've been bribing her with niceness ever since she got here –

SALESIO: What…?

LENA: – and we all know why.

She stuffs the roses into a wastepaper basket.

SALESIO: It's all very well for you, you're her aunt, you're part of the family. I don't relish the idea of being tossed out like an old sofa.

LENA: Serves you right.

SALESIO: Why are you always so unpleasant?

LENA: You sponged off her poor father for years.

SALESIO: That is not true.

LENA: And now you're siding with her sister.

SALESIO: What d'you mean, 'siding'?

LENA: What else would you call it?

SALESIO: She asked for my advice –

LENA: You should've had more faith.

SALESIO: Don't pretend you thought Cia was still alive –

LENA: I may've had some doubts, but only a very few.

SALESIO: – I remember you saying –

LENA: Doesn't matter what I said – I had no part in declaring her legally dead.

SALESIO: All I did was to fill in a few forms…

LENA: You behaved like a scoundrel. You *and* Ines.

SALESIO: Her father was my oldest friend, for heaven's sake. I was only trying to help the family.

LENA: Help yourself, you mean. Despicable. There's no other word for it. And then for Ines to put on a show of grief and weeping. Despicable. Thank God I'm not like her. At least I'm honest.

SALESIO: You may be honest, Lena, but you're damn ugly. Ugly in mind as well as body.

L'IGNOTA comes down the stairs. She has dressed in clothes that are the same as those in the wedding-day portrait.

LENA gasps with astonishment.

LENA: Cia! Dear child! You look just like –

SALESIO: The portrait! Astonishing.

LENA: Beautiful! Really beautiful!

SALESIO: Quite astonishing!

L'IGNOTA: I want to look the part if nothing else. What time are they coming?

SALESIO: Not for another hour or so. You look wonderful, my dear.

LENA: How are you feeling?

L'IGNOTA: Apprehensive.

SALESIO: But it's your own sister – her husband – they love you.

L'IGNOTA: My sister and her husband…! I couldn't have a more demanding audience. And I keep forgetting his name. The husband. Livio, is it Livio?

LENA: Silvio.

L'IGNOTA: Silvio! Silvio, Silvio. Did I know him before the war?

LENA: But of course.

SALESIO: He was a great friend of Bruno's. That's how he met Ines.

L'IGNOTA: Bruno has so many friends. I hope he doesn't expect me to remember them all.

LENA: Oh but surely – now that you're here – it'll all come back to you…

L'IGNOTA: Yes, yes, I'm sure it will. (*She walks to the balustrade and looks out at the landscape.*) How beautiful it is. Paradise. And what a glorious afternoon. (*She turns and looks at the portrait.*) It's very like me, don't you think?

LENA: (*Uncertain.*) Well, yes.

L'IGNOTA: Bruno said he had it painted from a photograph.

SALESIO: Yes, I think it was.

L'IGNOTA: And he told the painter all about me – every detail.

SALESIO: So he did.

LENA: To be honest, I've never liked that picture. I never thought it was – somehow – 'you'.

SALESIO: What on earth are you talking about?

LENA: It's the eyes. (*She goes to L'IGNOTA and gazes at her.*) Yes. These are her real eyes. The eyes I've always known.

(*Turning to the picture.*) Not those. Those aren't Cia's eyes. (*Looking at L'IGNOTA.*) Just the tiniest hint of green.

SALESIO: Blue – surely? – I call that blue.

L'IGNOTA: Green for Lena. Blue for Salesio. And for Bruno, grey – grey under black eyelashes. Look, you can see it in the portrait. That's what Bruno must've told the painter.

SALESIO: Well he got it wrong. I knew your father all his life – and you've got his eyes. Blue!

LENA: Nonsense! Ines has got his eyes. Don't pay any attention, Cia – you've got your mother's eyes – Green! – and I should know. We were girls together – two cousins with the same name.

SALESIO: Pretty Lena and –

He laughs.

LENA: Stop it, Salesio.

L'IGNOTA: What's the joke?

LENA: The boys used to tease us. They'd call after us down the street –

SALESIO: 'Pretty Lena – Ugly Lena!'

He is still laughing.

L'IGNOTA: (*A protest.*) No, no – not ugly!

LENA: I was never beautiful like your mother, but my heart was full of love. And when the pretty one died, this Lena, this 'ugly Lena' became a second mother to you. No one could've loved you more.

L'IGNOTA is moved by this.

L'IGNOTA: Dearest Lena.

LENA: All so long ago. (*A small smile.*) You really are the living image of your mother.

SALESIO: Her mother…?

LENA: It's quite remarkable.

SALESIO: She doesn't look like her mother at all.

LENA: Of course she does.

SALESIO: I don't agree.

LENA: You don't know what you're talking about.

SALESIO: I'm allowed my own opinion, aren't I? (*To L'IGNOTA.*) She's always so argumentative. (*L'IGNOTA laughs.*) What's the joke? What are you laughing at?

L'IGNOTA: These arguments. How you see me. How Lena sees me. How will *they* see me, I wonder – Ines

and Livio? As a long lost sister? A mysterious stranger?
A grasping impostor? It's like the plot of an absurd
melodrama.

LENA: They're just longing to see you. That's all that
matters.

SALESIO: It's Silvio, remember – not Livio.

L'IGNOTA: Silvio, Silvio, Silvio.

SALESIO: He's a lawyer, so you'd better be careful.

L'IGNOTA: Careful of what?

LENA glares at SALESIO, trying to silence him.

SALESIO: Well, he was the one who dealt with all that
legal, uh –

*He catches sight of LENA and stops in mid-sentence.
L'IGNOTA sees this.*

L'IGNOTA: All that legal what?

LENA: Nothing, my dear, nothing to worry about.

L'IGNOTA: Tell me.

LENA: (*Hissing.*) You fool, Salesio.

SALESIO: (*To LENA.*) I thought Bruno would've told her.

L'IGNOTA: Told me what?

LENA: Nothing of any importance.

L'IGNOTA: I want to know.

LENA: (*Lightly, referring to SALESIO.*) He's such a fool.

SALESIO: I'm sorry, Cia, but I assumed Bruno would've
told you about the, uh –

L'IGNOTA: About the what?

SALESIO: This villa. The estate. Didn't he explain?

L'IGNOTA: He said there'd been a quarrel. A legal problem. He said he didn't want to talk about it.

LENA: Quite right. Anyway, the situation's perfectly clear now.

SALESIO: Now that you're back.

LENA: Now that you're back safe and sound.

SALESIO: The Death Certificate'll be cancelled, annulled, whatever they call it.

L'IGNOTA: What Death Certificate…?

SALESIO: The one they issued when they thought you were dead.

LENA: (*To L'IGNOTA.*) It was a dreadful mistake – I blame Ines.

L'IGNOTA: Ines…?

LENA: They should never have done such a thing.

L'IGNOTA: It seems perfectly reasonable to me – if someone disappears for ten years it's reasonable to assume that she's dead.

SALESIO: (*To LENA.*) There – you see?

LENA: Well I was against it.

L'IGNOTA: Just a minute. Is this something to do with – ? (*Changing tack.*) – Bruno said all this belongs to me. Is that right?

SALESIO: Yes. It was a wedding present. From your late father.

L'IGNOTA: And if I were to die…?

SALESIO: It would go to your sister.

L'IGNOTA: To Ines…

LENA: To Ines.

SALESIO: Not that she wanted it, of course –

LENA: There you go! Taking her side again

SALESIO: (*To L'IGNOTA.*) They said I could live here. Ines and her husband. They said I could have my own apartment here. I'm an old man, no family, not many more years left.

L'IGNOTA: I see. (*She is standing very still, clearly disturbed by what she has been told.*) So as long I was missing – not dead – then Bruno, as my husband –

SALESIO: Kept the estate and the villa.

LENA: Yes, and he deserved to. You have no idea what it was like after the War. A heap of rubble. Bruno re-built it stone by stone.

L'IGNOTA: But it would've gone to Ines as soon as the death certificate was issued.

SALESIO: That's right.

LENA: Which is why your reappearance was such a shock.

L'IGNOTA: And Boffi knew this when he came to Berlin?

SALESIO: Of course.

LENA: Everyone was talking about it. People said Bruno refused to believe you were dead because he loved you so much.

SALESIO: Others said it was just a way of keeping the estate.

L'IGNOTA: Yes. I see.

LENA: Don't upset yourself, Cia. You're back, thank God. That's all that matters.

SALESIO: We won't mention it again.

LENA: Not another word.

L'IGNOTA: No, please, I want to talk about it. You see, in Berlin, Boffi told me he'd sent for Bruno as soon as he saw my photograph outside the nightclub.

LENA: And so he did – such excitement! – off he went on the very next train. It was a miracle. He couldn't wait to see you.

L'IGNOTA: Perhaps because – well, the death certificate had at last been issued, hadn't it? – so the estate was –

LENA: That had nothing to do with it.

L'IGNOTA: Are you sure?

LENA: Bruno always believed you were alive – always! And he recognised you straight away. As soon as he saw you.

L'IGNOTA: Did he?

LENA: Of course he did, you know he did.

L'IGNOTA: What about you?

LENA: (*Taken aback.*) Me…?

L'IGNOTA: Did you recognise me?

LENA: Well of course I did.

L'IGNOTA: The truth, please, Lena.

LENA: Well… (*She hesitates.*) Well, not straight away – I must confess – not immediately…

L'IGNOTA: Salesio…?

SALESIO: Not immediately, no.

LENA: It'd been a long time, after all – all those years…

SALESIO: No, it wasn't just that. Your manner, perhaps – something in your voice…

L'IGNOTA: You noticed a difference in my voice?

SALESIO: Yes, something…

L'IGNOTA: Boffi felt the same. He told me afterwards.

LENA: It's perfectly understandable. You were out of the country for so many years. Speaking a different language. You'd become – in a way – you'd become a different person.

L'IGNOTA: Perhaps Bruno thought that too…

SALESIO: Perhaps. Yes, it's possible.

LENA: Stop it, Cia. You're looking for trouble where none exists.

L'IGNOTA: Am I…?

LENA: Bruno was overwhelmed when he saw you. He told me. Overwhelmed. He said he wept.

L'IGNOTA: I wept too. I wept for myself. He embraced me. I let him embrace me. He called me Cia, Cia – his own darling Cia. He held me so tightly I could hardly breathe. He said he would take care of me, there was nothing to worry about, we would go back together and start our life all over again.

SALESIO: Which is what you did. Thank God.

LENA: He telephoned to say he was bringing you home.

L'IGNOTA: Home – yes.

LENA: We were all so excited.

L'IGNOTA: (*Almost to herself.*) 'Four months,' I said, 'give me four months – alone, with you – alone, in the villa – I need four months to become your Cia again.' And he promised.

LENA: He kept that promise.

L'IGNOTA: He did, yes. But now I find there's so much he hasn't told me – and I can't help wondering –

LENA: You must have faith in him, Cia. It's been difficult for Bruno – for all of us. People are astonished by your reappearance – astonished!

SALESIO: They're bound to ask questions.

L'IGNOTA: And I'm sure Boffi told them everything.

LENA: Oh no, I don't think –

L'IGNOTA: He must've done. He must've told them where he found me. (*To SALESIO.*) Didn't he? – nothing but a cheap cabaret singer – no better than a –

LENA: No, Cia, don't –

SALESIO: You mustn't pay attention to what people say –

L'IGNOTA: And what do they say? Do they say Bruno's taken me in because I can be useful to him?

LENA: No, no!

L'IGNOTA: I'm asking Salesio –

LENA: Nobody would ever think such a thing, let alone say it.

L'IGNOTA: (*To SALESIO.*) Tell me the truth. What do they say?

SALESIO: Well, yes, I suppose – certain things have been said –

L'IGNOTA: Tell me.

LENA: (*To SALESIO.*) Who? Who's been saying these things?

SALESIO: People – I can't remember who.

LENA Money, money, money – it all comes down to money.

SALESIO: (*To L'IGNOTA.*) You mustn't burden yourself with all these anxieties.

LENA: Bruno loves you. That's all that matters.

L'IGNOTA: Does he…?

LENA: You don't have to ask. You can see it in his face every time he looks at you.

L'IGNOTA: Yes, but when I first saw him – that evening in Berlin – I saw something else in his face. I saw a certain – disappointment.

SALESIO: Disappointment…?

L'IGNOTA: There was some sort of likeness – but not what he had hoped for. A resemblance, perhaps a strong resemblance – but no more. That's what I can't forget. That look of disappointment. It haunts me.

They stand very still, looking at each other.

The sound of an approaching car. LENA turns to the window.

LENA: A car!

SALESIO: It must be Ines and Silvio.

LENA: They're early. Why are they early?

SALESIO goes to the window.

SALESIO: No, it's Bruno. Boffi's with him. (*Calling.*) Bruno! Boffi! We're in here!

LENA: (*To L'IGNOTA.*) You mustn't blame Bruno.

L'IGNOTA: I'm not blaming anyone.

BRUNO enters with BOFFI. BRUNO is in his early forties: romantically handsome.

BRUNO: (*Brusquely, to L'IGNOTA.*) We've had another letter. (*To LENA and SALESIO, wanting them to leave.*) Would you mind…?

L'IGNOTA: Another letter?

BOFFI: From Berlin.

L'IGNOTA: What are you talking about?

BRUNO: Lena, Salesio – please. I need to talk to my wife.

SALESIO: Yes, of course. (*To LENA.*) Come along. (*To BRUNO.*) If you need us, we'll be upstairs.

LENA and SALESIO go. L'IGNOTA waits until they are out of earshot before she asks:

L'IGNOTA: What is it, Bruno? What's the matter?

BRUNO: We've had a letter from you friend. Your former friend.

L'IGNOTA: Salter…? What does he want?

BOFFI: He's making the most of not being dead.

BRUNO: He wants revenge.

BOFFI: He's on his way here.

BRUNO: And he's not alone.

L'IGNOTA: His daughter…!

BRUNO: No, not his daughter.

BOFFI: Remember what he said about a doctor he knew…?

L'IGNOTA: In Austria, yes.

BRUNO: Well he went to see him.

L'IGNOTA: Why? What for?

BRUNO: He's found some woman – a patient in this doctor's clinic. He says he's got proof.

L'IGNOTA: Proof of what?

BRUNO: That she – this woman – that she is Lucia. Not you.

L'IGNOTA: God.

BOFFI: And he's bringing her here.

BRUNO: Now. Today.

L'IGNOTA: Can't you stop him?

BRUNO: I'm sorry, Cia, it's all my fault. He wrote to me several times. I ignored him.

L'IGNOTA: That was a mistake.

BRUNO: Yes, yes, I see that now. He asked me to go to Vienna. He wanted me to talk to this doctor. And because I didn't reply…

L'IGNOTA: He's coming here.

BRUNO: Yes.

L'IGNOTA: Oh, Bruno.

BRUNO: I'm so sorry.

L'IGNOTA: Why didn't you tell me about this?

BRUNO: I didn't want to worry you. It seemed such a far-fetched story – this woman – a clinic in Vienna –

L'IGNOTA: You should've gone.

BRUNO: For what? Just to stare at some total stranger who doesn't look in the least like you?

L'IGNOTA: How do you know what she looks like?

BRUNO: He sent a photograph.

L'IGNOTA: Let me see…

BRUNO: I haven't got it.

BOFFI: He sent it to me.

L'IGNOTA: Why to you?

BOFFI: He wants me to show it to any other relatives and see if they recognise her.

BRUNO: The man's obsessed.

BOFFI: (*Continuing, to L'IGNOTA.*) I only got the photograph a few days ago. We didn't know what to do. Should we show it to Ines and Silvio? Should we go to Vienna, should we talk to Salter face to face?

BRUNO: Not a good idea, we thought.

BOFFI: *You* thought. That's what we should've done. We could've put an end to it, once and for all.

BRUNO: No, Boffi, it wouldn't have worked.

L'IGNOTA: So you decided to do nothing…

BRUNO: If people had found out we'd been to Vienna – you know what they're like – they'd've jumped to a hundred different conclusions –

L'IGNOTA: Oh, Bruno.

BRUNO: – all of them wrong.

L'IGNOTA: You're such an ostrich.

BRUNO: I thought it was for the best.

L'IGNOTA: And now he's coming here…

BRUNO: How was I to know he'd do that?

L'IGNOTA: And with proof, he says – what is it?

BRUNO: I've no idea.

BOFFI: Let's find out what train they're on.

L'IGNOTA: There's no point in doing that.

BOFFI: Why not? We can stop them coming to the house.

L'IGNOTA: You might avoid a disaster today – but what about tomorrow? It's a game Salter can play at any time.

BOFFI: What game?

L'IGNOTA: Unmasking the impostor. I have nothing to prove who I am.

BRUNO: You don't need any proof.

L'IGNOTA: Oh but I do. There are a thousand reasons for them to doubt what I say.

BRUNO: God! – I wish it was all over and done with!

L'IGNOTA: My darling Bruno – what's the worst thing that can happen? – you'll have been tricked – that's all – nothing more.

BRUNO: What do you mean?

L'IGNOTA: Tricked into believing that I was Cia. Just like Boffi. Just like Lena. Just like Salesio. You'll be in good company.

She laughs.

BOFFI: I'm glad you can laugh about it.

L'IGNOTA: Poor Bruno. Look at him. He finds it impossible to laugh – don't you? That's because you actually wanted – *needed* – to make the mistake – I didn't lead you into it.

BRUNO: Mistake? What mistake?

L'IGNOTA: Back me up, Boffi – I did everything I could, didn't I, to save him from falling into the – into the what? – into the trap I had set for him? Well, never mind. Here I am. I can answer for myself. But only for myself. I've been deceived too.

BRUNO: How? What do you mean?

L'IGNOTA: You know what I mean. (*To BOFFI.*) Go and meet Salter and this woman – the other me.

BOFFI: Then what?

L'IGNOTA: Bring them here.

BOFFI: Here…?

L'IGNOTA: Bring them here, Boffi. The more the merrier.

BOFFI: Are you sure?

L'IGNOTA: Bring them here.

BOFFI: Very well. If that's what you want.

BOFFI goes. Silence.

L'IGNOTA: Why didn't you tell me about Ines?

BRUNO: Ines…?

L'IGNOTA: The house, the estate, the death certificate.

BRUNO: I thought – I thought it'd upset you – I thought it'd cause even more problems.

L'IGNOTA: Facts, Bruno. They're the only real problem. Hard, immovable facts. You may think you can escape, soar like a bird above all the miseries and disappointments that life has heaped upon you – but in the end, you have to deal with the facts. They don't go away. Look at me, Bruno, look at me. I've been here – with you – for four months. (*She pulls him round to face her.*) Look at me, Bruno. Let me see myself in your eyes. Look at me, look at me! I've created myself in that image – the image I see gazing back at me in your eyes. That is now me – as you desire me. When I came here, I gave myself to you. 'Here I am,' I said, 'I am yours.' All my own memories have been blotted out. Give me yours, Bruno. Fill me with your memories. Fill me up. Let your memories come alive in me. Give me my life, Bruno!

BRUNO: Oh, Cia! – Cia!

L'IGNOTA: Yes, Cia – I am Cia! – You wanted me; now I exist! – You must believe that!

BRUNO: I do! – I swear to you! – I do believe!

L'IGNOTA: Do you? Do you really? When we're naked together, I've felt your hands on my body, searching – here (*Indicating a point above the hip.*) searching for what? – a birthmark you knew was there – but you haven't found it, have you? – it's not there – and so – because it's not there – what does that mean? Does it mean I'm not Cia? Does it? Or has the mark just disappeared? Or perhaps I had it removed. I didn't want it anymore. So I went to a clinic. I had it removed. And as we make love, I know you're looking for it – aren't you, Bruno?

BRUNO: Yes. Yes, you're right.

L'IGNOTA: And now you're terrified that Ines – with all her intimate sisterly knowledge – or Lena – with her bathtime memories of Cia's babyhood – might want to find that mark as the one final proof. 'But it's not there! How is that possible? How can something like that just disappear?' So they'll call in the doctors. And this other woman – does she have a mark on her hip? If she has it and I don't – what then? Would that be the end of everything? Oh, Bruno – my poor Bruno – don't

despair. I am Cia. I give you back the wife you long for
– I give her back to you so that I might live again myself
– live a life free of shame and humiliation. I am Cia – (*A
gesture to the painting.*) – not her – she is no longer alive
– I am Cia! – she lives in me!

The sound of a car approaching.

BRUNO: It's them! They're here!

L'IGNOTA: Go and meet them. I'll change these clothes. I
don't want them to see me like this. Hurry, Bruno – go
and meet them.

She hurries to the stairs.

BRUNO: (*As if imploring her.*) Cia…

*L'IGNOTA turns and looks at him. She speaks calmly and
with unshakeable confidence.*

L'IGNOTA: Yes. Cia!

She runs up the stairs.

Lights fade to black.

The shrill chirping of cicadas.

*Lights up. It is now evening and the landscape beyond the
loggia is veiled by purple shadows.*

*BRUNO and SALESIO are waiting with Cia's younger
(but older-looking) sister INES and her husband SILVIO
MÀSPERI. They are a smart sophisticated couple from
Milan.*

*INES is elegantly dressed, wearing a hat. She is smoking a
cigarette impatiently.*

*There is a long, still silence. Then LENA appears, walking
down the stairs.*

INES: So what exactly is happening?

LENA: She says she'll be down in a few minutes.

INES: She said that half an hour ago.

MÀSPERI: What precisely is she doing?

LENA: Standing in her bedroom surrounded by piles of clothes and suitcases.

INES: She's not leaving! Is she?

BRUNO: Of course not. She said she was going to change her dress.

LENA: Such a pity. She looked wonderful.

BRUNO: How is she?

LENA: I think she's been crying.

SALESIO: She's bound to be upset. Seeing everybody like this – quite an ordeal.

MÀSPERI: Ordeal? Why should it be an ordeal? Unless, of course, she bears a grudge against her sister. Do you think she does?

LENA: Absolutely not.

MÀSPERI: Are you sure?

BRUNO: If she's angry with anyone, it's me.

MÀSPERI: Ah! Well – if it's something between husband and wife…

He tails off discreetly.

INES: Is she resentful? Is that the problem?

LENA: She's not resentful in the least.

SALESIO: Not in the least, no. In fact she said this afternoon – didn't she, Lena? – this very afternoon – she said it was absolutely right – after ten years – to apply for a death certificate – (*To LENA.*) – isn't that what she said?

INES: I didn't do it for myself, Bruno. You know that. I have a daughter. It was because of her –

MÀSPERI: She must surely know we'd never do anything to hurt her.

SALESIO: Poor girl. The last thing she wanted was to find herself in the middle of a family quarrel.

BRUNO: What quarrel? Now she's back there's nothing to quarrel about.

LENA: That's what I told her.

INES: I wanted to come at once – (*To MÀSPERI.*) – didn't I? – I could've reassured her straightaway if only – if only Bruno hadn't –

MÀSPERI: That's right – if Bruno hadn't told us –

INES: (*To BRUNO.*) You said she didn't want to see anyone – least of all, me. It was very hurtful, Bruno. I know I could've convinced her that I never – I mean, never –

She covers her eyes with a handkerchief.

MÀSPERI: She knows that very well.

INES: I cried and cried for her.

MÀSPERI: It's obvious she understands what you did and why you did it. There's nothing to be upset about.

BRUNO: No, it's me. She didn't want to come here, and who can blame her? I mean – the past, all the

– everything that happened here – but I persuaded her – and I promised her in Berlin – I promised I wouldn't force her to see anyone. And I thought, well, give her time, wait until she's ready…

INES: But I could've reassured her –

BRUNO: It wasn't you, Ines –

INES: What, then?

BRUNO: I don't know. (*Glancing towards the stairs.*) What in God's name can she be doing?

INES: If she has no intention of coming down, there's precious little point in waiting.

LENA: Give her a little longer.

BRUNO: Go back and talk to her, Lena. Tell her she must come down.

INES: We've all waited far too long.

LENA: I'll do what I can.

LENA goes upstairs. INES sighs and lights another cigarette.

INES: This is very boring, Bruno. If she can't face seeing us this evening we might just as well go home. Really, so irritating. A complete waste of time.

MÀSPERI: We thought this was all cleared up. She can't go on bearing a grudge against Ines.

BRUNO: No, it's not that… There's something else.

MÀSPERI: Something else…? What?

BRUNO: Forgive me, Silvio, I just can't –

INES: Does Cia know?

BRUNO: Look, I can't handle this on my own. (*Going to the stairs.*) What *is* she doing? I need her here! (*LENA returns.*) Well…?

INES: Is she coming?

LENA: She says she'll wait till Boffi gets back.

BRUNO: For God's sake, Lena – what am I supposed to do?

LENA: I'm just telling you what she said.

BRUNO: This is ridiculous! What the hell is she playing at? – Cia! – Cia!

He runs up the stairs. INES turns to LENA.

INES: What's going on? Why is she doing this?

SALESIO: Something has happened.

LENA: Something we don't know about.

SALESIO: It's that letter.

MÀSPERI: What letter?

SALESIO: They got a letter from Berlin.

LENA: Earlier this afternoon.

SALESIO: Obviously bad news.

MÀSPERI: What sort of bad news?

LENA: They didn't say. Boffi was packed off to put a stop to whatever it was –

A car is heard approaching.

The beam of headlights sweeps across the room.

SALESIO: Here he is… (*Looking out.*) Yes, it's Boffi's car.

LENA: Let's hope she'll come down now.

SALESIO: He's not alone.

LENA: What?

SALESIO: There are two others. No, three!

They all look out.

MÀSPERI: It's a wheelchair!

LENA: And a woman.

INES: Is it a woman?

LENA: I think so.

BOFFI hurries in.

BOFFI: Where's Bruno? Where's Cia?

SALESIO: Upstairs.

BOFFI goes to the foot of the stairs.

BOFFI: Bruno! Bruno!

No response.

A NUN enters from the garden, pushing the MADWOMAN in a wheelchair. SALTER follows.

The MADWOMAN is fat and pale-skinned, with a waxen face, and expressionless eyes. There is always an empty meaningless smile on her lips. The NUN stands like a sentinel behind the wheelchair.

SALTER: Good evening.

Everyone stands and stares. The silence is broken by the MADWOMAN.

MADWOMAN: Le-na… Le-na…

LENA: Oh my God.

MADWOMAN: Le-na…

INES: How dreadful!

MADWOMAN: Le-na…

LENA: Is she calling me?

INES: Who is she?

MADWOMAN: Le-na…

LENA: Why is she –

SALTER: Are you a member of this family?

LENA: I am.

SALTER: Is your name Lena?

LENA: I'm Lena Cucchi. Cia's aunt.

SALTER: Well, well. A member of the family called Lena. That's something we didn't know.

MÀSPERI: Who are you? What are you talking about?

BOFFI: It's nothing. The woman keeps saying 'Lena' over and over again.

MADWOMAN: Le-na…

BOFFI: It's just a noise she makes..

MÀSPERI: Yes, but she *is* saying Lena.

BOFFI: (*Meaning CIA and BRUNO.*) Where the hell are they?

MÀSPERI: (*To BOFFI.*) What's going on? Why have you brought this woman here?

BOFFI ignores him; again he goes to the stairs and calls:

BOFFI: Bruno! Bruno! Come down!

SALTER: (*To BOFFI.*) Who are these people?

INES: I am Cia's sister.

BOFFI: This is her husband, Silvio Màsperi, and –

SALTER: (*Cutting in.*) The sister! Ah! So she has a sister.

INES: (*To SALTER.*) Who are you?

SALTER: My name is Salter, Carl Salter. Look at this unfortunate woman. Look at her, please.

INES: Look at her…?

BOFFI: He's convinced that she's –

SALTER: Don't you recognise her?

INES: Why should I?

SALTER: Because this is your sister.

MÀSPERI: What?!

INES: Cia…?

LENA: This woman…?

MADWOMAN: Le-na… Le-na…

SALTER: Yes, yes, this woman!

SALESIO: You're mad!

MADWOMAN: Le-na… Le-na…

SALTER: (*To LENA.*) Listen to her! She knows you.

INES: No!

SALTER: She's calling Lena. Don't you recognise her?

LENA: It's not possible.

SALTER: Look at her! Look at her eyes!

LENA: I don't believe it!

SALTER: A friend of mine in Vienna – a doctor – very experienced in these matters – has been studying her case for years. He has documents, proof…

MÀSPERI: What proof? Show us.

INES: No, no, this person is not my sister!

MÀSPERI: (*Referring to SALTER.*) Let him speak. If he has proof, let him tell us what it is.

INES: But Cia – my sister – she's upstairs…!

SALTER: Ah, yes – the lady upstairs. Yes, I know her well. All too well.

LENA: Not as well as I do. I was a second mother to her.

SALTER: No! – to this (*Indicating the MADWOMAN.*) poor woman here.

LENA: No, no, nonsense!

MÀSPERI: (*To SALTER.*) If you really have proof –

SALESIO: Lena's right. He's talking nonsense –

MÀSPERI: If this man thinks he has proof, the best thing is to –

SALESIO: – absolute rubbish!

MÀSPERI: – is to go to the proper authorities –

BOFFI: He's doing this for a reason – and I know what it is. So do Bruno and Lucia. Where are they?

MÀSPERI: So what is this reason?

SALTER: (*Referring to BOFFI.*) He calls it revenge.

BOFFI: Ex-actly! Precisely!

SALTER: I call it punishment.

SALESIO: (*To SALTER.*) If you've got proof, let's see it.

LENA: Otherwise people will start taking advantage –

INES: Nobody's taking advantage of anyone. You shouldn't say things like that. (*To SALTER.*) Now look. Everyone in this room – me, Lena, Salesio – Boffi – we've all known Cia for the whole of our lives – and not one of us – not one of us – has recognised this poor woman.

SALTER: Is that because you've already recognised the lady upstairs?

INES: Well no, not exactly.

SALTER: You mean you didn't recognise her?

INES: I mean I haven't seen her.

SALTER: (*Astonished.*) You haven't…?

INES: I came here today from Milan in order to see her. I haven't done so yet.

SALTER: But why have you waited? Are you saying you've deliberately avoided seeing her?

INES: No, no, of course not.

SALTER: She's been here four months.

INES: Yes, I know, it was she who –

SALTER: (*Finishing the sentence for her.*) She who didn't want to see you.

INES: She wanted time alone with Bruno.

SALTER: Of course! Yes, I see. I understand completely. How could she possibly deceive a sister? Impossible! She couldn't do it. She's no fool, the lady upstairs. She knows you'd know – the touch of her cheek against yours – you'd *feel*… (*Turning to the MADWOMAN.*) But this lady – touch her –

INES: No!

SALTER: embrace her –

INES: No!

SALTER: you will know then – for an absolute certainty – that this is your sister.

INES: No – no, I can't!

SALTER: Have pity, Signora. Think of the ten years that have passed since you last saw her face. Think of what she has suffered, think of it. The hunger, the terror, the brutality, the abuse. Think of it. I know the woman upstairs claims to be your Cia. But look carefully at this lady – look beneath the ravages of those years. Look at her – look at her! It is Cia's face you see.

INES: No – no!

SALTER: Look at her eyes.

INES: Lifeless.

SALTER: Look at the colour of her eyes.

MADWOMAN:Le-na – Le-na –

INES: The colour – well, yes, the colour is similar.

MÀSPERI: (*To SALTER.*) How did you find this woman?

SALTER: It was many years ago. She was found wrapped in an army coat – an infantryman's coat – torn and stained – but there was a badge…

MÀSPERI: What badge?

LENA: Where was she found?

SALTER: At Lintz.

MÀSPERI: What sort of badge?

SALTER: The badge of the German regiment that was stationed here – here – right here!

MÀSPERI: During the war?

SALTER: Yes.

BOFFI: That proves nothing!

SALESIO: Somebody might've given her the coat.

LENA: Out of pity.

MADWOMAN: Le-na… Le-na…

SALTER: She calls for Lena all the time. And why is that? (*To LENA.*) 'I was a second mother to her.' Your words.

LENA goes to the MADWOMAN and cradles the woman's face in her hands.

LENA: Cia! Cia! Cia!

L'IGNOTA appears at the top of the stairs. BRUNO is with her. L'IGNOTA looks at the scene in front of her.

L'IGNOTA: Why don't you all try calling her? See which one she answers.

SALTER: Ah. Here she is.

L'IGNOTA: Yes, Salter – here I am.

INES: Cia…!

L'IGNOTA walks down the staircase.

The room is full of shadows. A tiny cluster of lights in a distant village can be seen in the landscape beyond the garden.

L'IGNOTA: Let's have some light in here. Nobody can see anything.

SALESIO switches on the lights.

INES: Cia…

SALTER: Is it Cia? Are you sure?

L'IGNOTA: (*To SALTER, as she looks around.*) This whole scene – this 'performance' – stinks of your cruelty, Salter.

She goes to the MADWOMAN, and with compassionate delicacy she places her fingers under the MADWOMAN's chin to look more closely at her vacantly smiling face.

MADWOMAN: Le-na…

L'IGNOTA: (*Taken aback.*) Lena…?

The MADWOMAN seems to turn towards LENA.

SALTER: There, you see?

INES: She's looking at Lena.

BOFFI: (*To IGNOTA.*) She says 'Lena' all the time. It's meaningless, like a vocal tic.

SALTER: Yes, but she turned and looked at the Signora.

L'IGNOTA: And that's enough, is it? That's all the proof you need? I know you (*Addressing SALTER.*) don't believe me – but as I came down the stairs I caught you (*Indicating LENA.*) bending over that poor creature and calling her 'Cia – Cia…'!

LENA: Only because he –

SALESIO: (*Overlapping.*) He insisted!

BOFFI: (*Overlapping.*) The woman was calling 'Le-na – Le-na'…

L'IGNOTA: (*Decisively, louder.*) Yes, yes, yes, there's an explanation for everything. (*To LENA.*) I saw how you looked at me just now.

LENA: How I looked…?

L'IGNOTA: (*To SALESIO.*) You too…

SALESIO: Me? Never!

L'IGNOTA: And you, Boffi.

BOFFI: Not true, not true! Nobody has recognised her.

SALESIO: We're all so, uh –

BOFFI: Your own sister – when she saw you –

L'IGNOTA: Yes, she called me Cia.

BOFFI: Twice!

L'IGNOTA: Yes, twice.

BOFFI: (*To SALTER.*) You heard her, didn't you? (*Turning to MÀSPERI.*) Even you…

INES: Nobody in this room wants to take advantage.

LENA: No, no, of course not, I was just pointing out –

BOFFI: Bruno, for God's sake say something.

L'IGNOTA: What can he say? Just look at him, poor boy.
Totally bewildered.

BRUNO: No, astonished – astonished by this man's
(*Meaning SALTER.*) unbelievable nerve. If anyone's
taking advantage of the situation, it's him.

L'IGNOTA: Don't worry, he's not going to take advantage
of anyone – not of me, not of this poor woman –

SALTER: It's not a question of taking advantage, I felt it
was my duty –

L'IGNOTA: To bring her here.

SALTER: To punish you.

L'IGNOTA: To punish me…?

SALTER: I nearly died because of you – it was you who
took advantage – you came here to trick and deceive –

L'IGNOTA: I've tricked nobody.

SALTER: Just as you did with me. You've tricked and
deceived and cheated –

BRUNO: (*Advancing towards SALTER.*) How dare you!

L'IGNOTA: It's all right, Bruno, I can handle him.
(*Going to SALTER.*) You say I've tricked and deceived
and cheated. And what is your proof? This poor
sick woman. Well done, Salter. It looks as if you've
succeeded.

BOFFI: Succeeded…?

L'IGNOTA: Creating doubt.

LENA: Never!

BOFFI: (*Overlapping.*) Nonsense!

SALESIO: Nobody doubts for a moment –

L'IGNOTA: I saw your faces.

SALESIO: But we didn't recognise her!

BOFFI: None of us.

SALESIO: Not for a moment.

BOFFI: Not for a single moment – I've never doubted you –

L'IGNOTA: Oh but you did. You had to persuade yourself by reminding us that Ines had twice called me Cia.

LENA: And so she did.

BOFFI: This is ridiculous! – how could I possibly have any doubts about you because of this poor wretch –

L'IGNOTA: Not because of her – because of *me*. It doesn't matter that you don't recognise her. Your doubts are completely natural. Me, appearing out of nowhere – of course you were confused. (*Turning to LENA.*) Don't cry, Lena. There's nothing on this earth, no belief, no conviction, that can resist the serpent of doubt when it slithers into your mind – and once it has, your belief can never be the same again.

SALTER: So it's possible you're not Cia? – you admit that?

L'IGNOTA: I admit a great deal more. This woman might indeed be Cia – if that's what they believe.

BRUNO: But we don't believe that!

BOFFI: None of us!

SALTER: Why not?

BRUNO: Well, because –

SALTER: Because she (*Indicating L'IGNOTA.*) looks like the Cia you want, and she (*Indicating the MADWOMAN.*) does not…?

L'IGNOTA: No, no, not because I look like her! I've told everyone – I told them, Salter – physical likeness is no proof of anything. In fact, the reverse is more likely – how could anyone who has suffered so much during the last ten years look so unchanged?

MÀSPERI: That's true – I never thought –

L'IGNOTA: Yes, Signor Màsperi, it *is* true – (*To SALTER.*) You see…? Slither, slither – the serpent's doing his job.

BRUNO: This is ridiculous! You're doing everything possible to undermine –

L'IGNOTA: You've had the same thoughts, Bruno.

BRUNO: Never! When?

L'IGNOTA: In Berlin. When that door opened and you found me again. I could see you were shaken by what you saw. Understandably. But when you believe in someone – or need to believe – then you dismiss such uncomfortable thoughts.

BRUNO: You're deliberately trying to make everyone doubt you.

L'IGNOTA: I am, you're right (*Indicating the MADWOMAN.*) You haven't recognised her. Is that because she's unrecognisable? Or perhaps – and I think this is nearer the truth – you don't want to believe what you really see. And yet… Hundreds of wretched people have come back like her – unrecognisable, minds and memories a blank – sisters, brothers, fathers, mothers have fought over them – 'She's mine, she's mine – no, she's mine!' – not because she looked like their own flesh and blood – but because they *wanted* to believe. Doesn't matter about proof. Doesn't even matter about common sense. If you need to believe in something enough, then you believe it. Look at me. You believed in me without a shred of evidence.

BRUNO: You *are* Cia.

BOFFI: We didn't need any evidence.

L'IGNOTA: That's not true. Look at Signor Màsperi – (*To MÀSPERI.*) – doubt and suspicion written all over your face –

MÀSPERI: No, no –

L'IGNOTA: – and I don't blame you. It was so very convenient my turning up when I did.

BRUNO: Convenient for me – is that what you mean?

L'IGNOTA: As soon as the death certificate was issued, Cia returns. Perfect timing. (*To MÀSPERI.*) I've been here four months – comfortable, well looked-after, cared for, loved even – and during that time I've made myself into her – I said I couldn't bear to see anyone – too upsetting – a good excuse, don't you think? – (*To BRUNO.*) – and very useful for you, my darling.

BRUNO: I knew it, I knew it! – that's what you believed all along!

L'IGNOTA: (*To INES and MÀSPERI.*) It was easy when I came here to pretend I didn't want to awaken painful memories – it was easy to pretend I'd forgotten everything – and all the time creating and storing a past life. I needed time – as he (*Indicating BRUNO.*) needed time – rebuilding the villa stone by stone – I was doing the same with Cia – transforming her memories into my memories – little by little, until I felt I could greet my beloved sister (*Going to INES, arms outstretched.*) and talk to her about the childhood we had shared – the happy days we spent together – two little orphans brought up by a devoted aunt. I made myself into Cia – I became her – as if I had stepped down from that portrait. I even had her dress copied –

LENA: (*Pointing to the painting.*) That dress.

L'IGNOTA: I had it copied, Ines. I was going to greet you – standing here – in that dress – then I thought, no, no – too much. (*Turning to MÀSPERI.*) Surely now, Signor Màsperi – surely now those little wriggling doubts are becoming something more substantial…?

MÀSPERI: I don't know what to say.

INES: Who would ever think of doing such a thing?

L'IGNOTA: Ask Bruno.

BRUNO: It's just not true!

L'IGNOTA: And now – look at him! – terrified that this suspicion – the suspicion I myself have created – may turn out to be truth.

BRUNO: Stop this! I don't believe a word of it. None of us do.

L'IGNOTA: That's where you're wrong. They do believe it. All of them.

BOFFI: But Signora…!

L'IGNOTA: It's certainly what he (*A gesture to SALTER.*) believes to be true.

BRUNO: (*To L'IGNOTA.*) If this is your revenge – well, it's even more brutal than his.

L'IGNOTA: Not *my* revenge, darling Bruno – the revenge of facts! The facts are taking their revenge. The truth is – I don't give a damn whether these people recognise me or not. Not a single solitary damn. You're the one who should recognise me, Bruno, and you're not sure. That is the fact.

BRUNO: For God's sake, Cia – I know you're doing this to test me! Stop it! Stop it!

L'IGNOTA: No Bruno, I'm not.

BRUNO: Yes, yes – that must be the reason! That is not what I believe.

L'IGNOTA: I'll tell you what to believe. Believe I'm a cheat – a fraud – an impostor. Believe what Salter tells you. Believe that he is right – and this poor creature may be – she may be – possibly – probably is – your very own Cia. Look at her…

She goes to the MADWOMAN, gently raising the woman's chin and gazing into her eyes.

MADWOMAN: Le-na…

L'IGNOTA: (*Turning to LENA.*) There! – she's calling you – why don't you believe it?

MADWOMAN: Le-na…

L'IGNOTA: You see? It's you she's calling for. She comes here calling 'Lena, Lena' – she calls and calls – and you won't believe her. Why not? (*She gazes at the*

MADWOMAN.) Listen to her voice. Look at the smile on her lips. (*She speaks to the MADWOMAN*.) Where are you?

MADWOMAN Le-na…

L'IGNOTA: Somewhere far away, I think – marooned for ever, but safe. Immune.

MADWOMAN: Le-na – Le-na…

As if guided by some strange attraction or instinct, LENA approaches the MADWOMAN, but then draws back; L'IGNOTA observes this.

L'IGNOTA: Go to her, Lena.

LENA: No, I…

L'IGNOTA: Stay with her. She needs you. (*She turns and looks at SALTER*.) Why are you smiling?

SALTER: Am I smiling?

L'IGNOTA: Salter: you're worthless. A worthless human being and a worthless writer.

SALTER: Well, yes, that's a possibility…

L'IGNOTA: Everything about you is despicable.

SALTER: Again – that's possible.

L'IGNOTA: You're like your books. Cold and cynical. No trace of compassion or humanity.

SALTER: But rich.

L'IGNOTA: (*Ignoring this*.) You don't know what it is to suffer – to really suffer. That's why you have no understanding –

SALTER: Of what?

L'IGNOTA: Of a despair so deep and terrible that it makes you take revenge on life by destroying the past. And when the chance is offered, when you try to create a new life – a life that is happier, better – life as it should be – you (*Meaning SALTER.*) assume that my motives are the same as yours – and because we were together for a few years, you assume I'm a money-grubbing fake like you.

SALTER: And you've put your heart into this, have you? – no money-grubbing fakery for you...

L'IGNOTA: Oh, Salter – what's the point of trying to explain anything? You wouldn't believe me.

SALTER: I might. This is a charming villa, after all – and I'm sure your life here has been very pleasant. Perfectly understandable.

L'IGNOTA: And you think that's why I did it...?

SALTER: Why not?

L'IGNOTA: Some things are done for different reasons. It depends on how you react to misfortune. Look at that poor woman. (*Indicating the MADWOMAN.*) Imagine what might've happened to her. Seized here – in this villa, this very room, perhaps – seized with a ferocity and a brutality that's hard to believe – seized and raped over and over again. Violated, defiled, driven – forced into madness. No hope of redemption. A life sentence without remission. But there's another sort of madness – the hell I shared with you in Berlin.

SALTER: (*Tense, warning her.*) If this a game, stop it now.

L'IGNOTA: (*Ignoring him.*) Imagine this villa, this room, as it was just before the War – two sisters, alone, the youngest just eighteen years old – untouched by life, on the morning of her marriage – so innocent, God, so painfully innocent… (*As she speaks L'IGNOTA moves closer and closer to INES.*) …clinging tightly – never wanting to leave her sister – weeping, not because she didn't love the man she was about to marry – no, not because of that, Silvio – but because, in her innocence, she knew nothing – nothing! And how could she? She had no mother. 'I'm so frightened' – the sister was crying as she spoke – 'he'll want to touch me – to put his hands on my body – he'll hurt me' –

INES gasps.

INES: Nobody – nobody else knows that!

BRUNO: (*To L'IGNOTA.*) Who told you? Who?

L'IGNOTA: Only a sister could know something so secret, so intimate.

INES: Yes!

L'IGNOTA: Sister to sister.

INES: Yes, yes! Cia, oh Cia, forgive me for doubting you.

L'IGNOTA does not respond directly; she turns to SALTER:

L'IGNOTA: You feel so dirty, so encrusted with filth, you think you'll never get clean again – and you go off – drifting on the tide of war until, eventually, you end up in Berlin – you learn to sing, you learn to dance, you learn to trade on your looks and live on your wits – and there's applause and admirers – men like you, Salter, lots of them, and you do anything and everything – and then, one night, out of the darkness, somebody calls to you – a strange-looking man, like the devil – 'Signora Lucia, your husband is here, just round the corner, let me fetch him – Lucia, Lucia!' – and I thought – what did I think? – I thought this poor man, this 'husband', he's searching for someone who doesn't exist – but he could create that someone in me – not as *I* am (for I'm just a clean slate, a tabula rasa) – but as *he* wished, as he desired me. (*To SALTER.*) And you, Salter – you've come all this way to punish me for my fraud and deception – but was it a fraud, was it deception…? Well, you stopped me in the nick of time. Do you know what I was going to do? Can you guess? I was going to have myself recognised by my sister and my brother-in-law – the stamp of family approval – two strangers, two people whom I've never seen before.

INES: Cia…

L'IGNOTA: Or perhaps I have.

INES: Darling Cia – what are you saying? You've just proved –

L'IGNOTA: I've proved nothing. I've never been to this place until Bruno brought me.

BRUNO: That's not true – please tell me it's not true!

L'IGNOTA: How can I? I have no memory. (*Going to BRUNO.*) Dear Bruno. I wanted you to believe I was Cia. And for a time I was. I believed it too. Almost. But now this Cia's going away, going back to Berlin to dance and to sing and to fuel the erotic fantasies of old men in cabaret clubs.

BRUNO: What…?!

L'IGNOTA: I'm going to Berlin with Salter. (*To SALTER.*) You've won!

BRUNO: You can't! I know you're Cia! You've proved it! I forbid you to go! This is where you belong!

He takes her by the arm, but she pushes him away. They stand facing each other.

L'IGNOTA: When you rebuilt the villa you should've looked through the rubble to see if there was something of hers that had been left behind – something of her spirit, perhaps, a memory, something still alive – something she, and only she, would know about. I looked. I found it. Up in the attic there was an old sandalwood cabinet. Battered and scratched, with little silver insects stuck to the door. It was a miracle that it survived. And in one of the drawers, I found a notebook. Cia's notebook. She'd written the words that Ines had spoken on the morning of her wedding. 'I'm so frightened – he'll want to touch me – to put his hands on my body – he'll hurt me.'

BRUNO: I don't believe it. Where is this notebook? Let me see it.

L'IGNOTA: No. It's mine now. Finders keepers. (*A small smile.*) The strange thing is: the handwriting – it looks just like mine. Come along, Salter! (*She turns to leave, but pauses.*) Something else I meant to say. Ines: look on this poor woman's hip. I think you'll find –

SALTER: A birthmark. The doctor told me.

L'IGNOTA: A red mark.

SALTER: Black. Like an insect.

L'IGNOTA: It must've darkened with age. In the notebook it says: 'a red birthmark on my hip – like a ladybird'. (*To BRUNO.*) That's what you were looking for, isn't it? More proof! She's the one. You must believe it now. (*To SALTER as she goes to the door.*) Let's go. Before I change my mind.

SALTER: (*Triumph.*) You won't change your mind!

BRUNO: How can you be so sure?

SALTER: You offer a romantic dream. I offer certainty. It may be a brutal certainty, but at least she can rely on it. And that, my friend, is what people want. (*To L'IGNOTA.*) Are you ready?

L'IGNOTA: I am. (*To BOFFI.*) Send my things to Berlin. You know the address.

SALTER: (*Going.*) Come on – let's go!

L'IGNOTA: Wait, wait, I'm coming! (*She follows him, pausing momentarily to speak to BRUNO.*) La commedia è finita!

L'IGNOTA goes.

BRUNO: No, Cia, no! – you can't leave us! (*Running after them.*) Cia! Cia!

BRUNO goes, followed by BOFFI, SALESIO, INES and MÀSPERI.

BRUNO can be heard calling 'Cia! Cia!'. Then the sound of a car engine.

Headlights sweep across the shadow-filled garden.

The room is in darkness now. LENA is left alone with the MADWOMAN and the NUN.

MADWOMAN: Le-na…

LENA: (*An incredulous whisper.*) Cia…!

Lights fade to black.